Feeling inspired?

Check out these other HarperTrue titles:

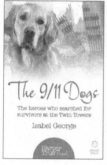

RAW

The diary of an anorexic

Lydia Davies

HarperTrueLife
An imprint of HarperCollins*Publishers*
1 London Bridge Street
London SE1 9GF

www.harpertrue.com
www.harpercollins.co.uk

First published by HarperTrueLife 2015

© Lydia Davies 2015

Lydia Davies asserts the moral right to be
identified as the author of this work

A catalogue record of this book is
available from the British Library

ISBN: 978-0-00-814696-2

Printed and bound in Great Britain by
CPI Group (UK) Ltd, Croydon, CR0 4YY

MIX
Paper from
responsible sources
FSC™ C007454

10 March 2014

At the age of 19 I was diagnosed with anorexia nervosa. Through this illness, I lost so much more than just an excessive amount of weight. I was ripped away from the life I had created at university in Newcastle, thus taking away my degree, two and a half years' worth of work, my freedom, friends, boyfriend and independence. I was transported back to the life a child lives, being nursed, cared for and catered to by my incredible family. Every sense of normality in life that I knew was gone, and so was my sanity.

The pages that follow are a raw record of the unexpected journey I found myself on. Along with original letters from my doctors, I have included letters to and from family members and friends, messages of support and encouragement from loads of amazing people when I was really struggling, posts from my blog which I wrote throughout my attempts at recovery, personal notes from my phone and suicide notes that I wrote in desperate times.

The first letter from my mother is, I now realise, the starting point of when my secret

Lydia Davies

(which I didn't know I had) was out. I was in complete denial, and absolutely oblivious to the fact that I was anorexic. To be looked in the eye and told by a medical professional that you are going to die should be one of the most terrifying moments imaginable. When I was told this on three separate occasions, not once did it hit me. I was so far away in a separate realm to reality that my concept of everything was gone.

Two years on, what happened to me is still extremely raw, and it consumes a large space of my mind, dominating most of my memories. Through recovery I developed bulimia nervosa, attempted suicide on more occasions than I would like to mention, have been at my absolute lowest mentally and physically, and ripped my family's hearts out.

This chronological map of words and documents may help people to understand the damaged and delicate mind of a sufferer. I want people to be informed about what it is really like to get pulled down so deep into the dangerous world of disordered eating, and I want other sufferers to feel comfort, and perhaps gain courage from this open book of my most personal secrets.

19 October 2011

It was on the nineteenth of October 2011 that I received a letter from my mother via email, which cut through my heart like a knife. My stomach dropped and I burst into tears as I read it. I had been completely emotionless and glassy-eyed for some time up until this point.

A letter from my mum

Dear Lydia,

From the moment you were born I loved you with all my heart and that love has only deepened with time. You are beautiful, smart, funny, kind, loyal, caring . . . (and many more good things). You have so much going for you: loyal friends who love you, a lovely boyfriend, a family who loves you (you mean the world to all of us). You have a great living situation this year and you seem to be getting stuck into work in a more positive way than last year or the year before. It is lovely hearing you sound positive and excited about the future, thinking of Paris, styling, travelling, etc.

Lydia Davies

You were brave in seeking help for feelings of depression in the summer and while the positive effects of the treatment are clear to see, it will be natural to have ups and downs – everyone does; but keeping on with the counselling will, as you know, help you to deal with negative thoughts.

I have written hundreds of letters to you in my head when I can't sleep for worrying about you, and I thought that I would try to write some of my worries down, because I can't store all this up in my head for much longer.

Although you seem to be feeling a bit happier, you are continuing to get thinner and thinner. Everyone can see that you have an eating disorder and that you need help to get better – except you can't see it. It is not your fault and you probably can't help it – that is what this illness is like. If you can't see how frighteningly thin you have become, then think about how you feel. Cold? Tired? Aching body? Low energy? etc. Is this how you want to spend the rest of your life? You don't have to. This flu and its complications are not surprising. Your defences will not be able to fight off germs as your immune system has been compromised. You used to read a lot of stuff about illnesses that you thought you might have. Well, now that you have this, I wonder if you have looked up any information about it. There are some useful websites, e.g.

- b-eat.co.uk
- ABC anorexiabulimiacare.org.uk
- Supportline.org.uk/problems/anorexia.php

Effects of a starvation diet:

I think you already know some of the long-term effects, e.g.

- Body metabolizes/eats its own muscle to stay alive (this is happening to you now).
- Can lead to heart disease or even heart attack.
- Osteoporosis/bone-wasting disease – all the minerals are leached out of your bones, causing them to become brittle and fragile and break easily. Also, you shrink and I can see that your posture has changed; you have become hunched. If this is left to continue, your body will sadly become more like that of a frail 90-year-old woman than a 20-year-old.
- Loss of periods/fertility – if not corrected early enough, you may never know the joy of creating a family with someone you love. This would be so sad.
- Dry skin, pale yellowy complexion, dry brittle hair which then starts to fall out, fine downy hair growing on the face and body . . . the list goes on . . .

If left untreated you will get worse and worse until you are hospitalised. I don't want that and I'm sure you don't either.

The thing is, Lydia, that you can choose to continue along this path or to turn things around and to get better. I know it must seem a very hard step to take – to firstly admit that you have a problem and then to say that you want to get better (to someone, anyone, a doctor?). There is lots of help out there but you need to want it. You are a strong person and I hope and pray that you will have the courage to seek this help ASAP and to take control in turning your life around for the better. It won't be easy (the hardest thing will be the first step) but you will have us all and your friends to support you. Everybody wants you to get better. The sooner proper professional treatment begins, the better the outcome.

Please, please, please, I beg you (we all do), please want to get better.

I will always love you,

Mum xoxoxox

I discovered that a housemate across the hall from me had electronic scales in her bedroom. I had never owned scales – my mother believed it could be unhealthy (as it is just a number,

Raw

which is irrelevant). This machine fascinated me. When everyone was out of the house I found myself sneaking into her room more and more frequently to step on this incredible glass square. It started out as once a week, or every few days, out of curiosity. This quickly turned into me darting in and out just to see what number it would read at every opportunity I got. I was addicted to seeing the numbers drop. If they had not dropped or had gone up by even a quarter of a pound I would burst into tears, try to be sick or do some star jumps, and then consult the scales again literally half an hour later, praying that they would have gone down. I remember getting below the 7-stone mark and feeling absolutely triumphant. I had never in my life felt more proud of myself than I did then. The last time I had weighed myself properly was years before, and I had been 9 stone plus. I was absolutely buzzing, and determined to get my weight down further and further.

6 November 2011

Email from a friend

Lydia you look hungry! You would look so much nicer with a bitta weight on you x x

My identity became my eating disorder, and my eating disorder was my identity. I looked in the mirror and could not believe how thin I had got. I gazed at my perfect legs, ran my blue fingers over my protruding ribcage like a piano. My face was sunken, my cheekbones like daggers. The largest part of my body was my haunted eyes, which stared back at me in the mirror in a state of pure amazement and triumph at what I had achieved. I bought a pair of size-four jeans which dangled around my stick-like legs, and hung so loose around my waist and bottom that I had to wear three pairs of tights and a pair of leggings under them just to keep them on. My hip bones poked out through my clothes, my stomach was concave and my elbows sharp as knives. My breasts were completely non-existent, and even

Raw

a child's bra sat inches away from my chest. Even my knickers didn't fit, as I no longer had a bottom. They hung limply off me and resembled a loose nappy. Yes, to you this may all sound extremely unattractive, but I felt absolutely stunning. I did not look real, I looked like some strange mystical creature, and that is what I felt like, on a trip away with the fairies, deep in a world of fantasy. In contrast, though, I felt fearful. Fearful of death at times, but then when I was feeling euphoric I could not care less. Such a mix of these powerfully contrasting feelings is almost impossible to describe unless you have been through this yourself. Even then, though, I cannot say that other people felt the same. The beautifully haunted world that I was living in was miles away from anyone else and everything else.

18 November 2011

From my GP in Newcastle

I have been seeing Lydia at the Eating Disorder Unit since the beginning of October. For some time Lydia has struggled with anxiety and depression and has been restricting her diet in order to lose weight. In the last four weeks she has been seen and assessed by our Regional Eating Disorder Unit and has been diagnosed with anorexia nervosa. Lydia is undertaking a community based treatment programme and her mum has moved up to Newcastle to support her with this. The Eating Disorder Consultant is doing this as a trial over the next couple of weeks but it may come to a point where Lydia has to be admitted to an inpatient bed in the Eating Disorder Unit in Newcastle. Lydia is currently attending the Eating Disorder Unit twice a week to have bloods, heart tracing and weight assessments. She is following a strict diet treatment plan.

Yours sincerely,

Dr * *******

Raw

Both my parents came to my consultation with the head psychiatrist at the Eating Disorder Unit. She was a large, fearsome-looking woman whom I immediately decided I hated. She led me through the inpatient unit to assess me. On the way through, we passed several demented-looking skeletons. I gasped at how thin and emaciated they looked (unaware that to others I looked much the same). As sick and twisted as it sounds, I felt jealous of them. I also felt embarrassed to be there. They must all be wondering who this fat girl is and why she is here – she doesn't have anorexia! Funnily enough, we were all probably thinking the same thing about each other, eyes darting, analysing and comparing our bodies to each other's in a swift glance. Sizing up the 'competition'.

4 December 2011

My blog post

Influence and Inspiration

I have decided to make this blog more of a personal diary of my thoughts, and use it for myself to look back on, though if you happen to read it I hope that you gain some inspiration and enjoyment . . .

My family. They are absolutely amazing and I am so grateful.

My boyfriend. Equally amazing.

My friends. And again . . .

Listening to wise people.

One night we went to a bar to sell our goods. I put on my sparkly high heels, baggy leggings and a jumper. I felt like I finally looked pretty amazing. My legs were like two pins (they were more like needles). I got drunk and had a lovely evening. I had a conversation with one of my lecturers who attended that night and it inspired me so much. She told me it was great that I had come out but I needed to sort myself out. She said she had wanted to bring me vitamin drinks into university on several occasions, because if I wasn't going to eat I could at least drink. We talked about ways in which to inspire myself through glamour and fashion. She told me to watch old movies and escape through reading and ideas. It was an amazing conversation and it lit a lightbulb in my head. I confided in her and explained how I didn't know who I was any more. Our conversation hit the right nerve and I will remember it forever.

4 December 2011

My blog post

Something I wrote in my phone, probably at 5.40 a.m.,
one time:

The worst thing is having to think about it and talk about it
all the time. Having fun, being creative, listening to inspiring
people and watching inspiring films can take me away. Drawing,
ink, outfits, glamour, ideas, aspirations are a saviour. Confidence,
influence and inspiration are key words. Nothing is safe but
everything is amazing. Creativity and drive will save me.
Excitement and networking and listening to and hearing
other people.

**The only way in which I was able to warm up my
permanently icy body was by sitting in a bath full
of boiling water. I would run it as deep as I could
before the water started to get cold. Actually,
getting in was horrendous, as it meant taking
off all of my clothes and being unbearably cold
for some long seconds. I would lower myself in
slowly until my sharp tailbone clunked against**

the bottom of the tub. It was absolute agony to sit. I would lie back, my spine cracking against the surface. Sometimes I would exhale all of the air in my lungs and lie completely under the water, just to see what it might feel like to not be in the world any more. I would imagine drowning and only bring myself back up when I had to. I would look down at my purple knees, and would examine my skeleton of a body. Sometimes I would stroke the layer of fur that was developing on my arms, and wonder whether I HAD taken things too far, and even be a little scared. Thoughts like this never lasted more than a few seconds, as they quickly disappeared behind the mist of the voice congratulating me for achieving skinny. Getting out of the bath was dreadful. Being soaking wet and THAT cold was excruciating. I would dart to my bedroom down the hall and blast the hairdryer over my transparent skin in a desperate attempt to heat myself again.

Another thing I did a lot around this time was sit on benches. I would just walk around completely dazed and sit on benches anywhere by myself, and not think. I would be completely blank and glazed over, but horrendously lonely, cold and depressed at the same time. I remember sitting on a bench in town outside a church for several hours once. I was completely numb, and feeling nothing, till I felt a tear slide down my face, and then another, and then another. I didn't move, I just sat there, blinking terrified tears, but feeling powerless to them. I felt like I had nowhere to go, no one to talk to and nothing to say anyway. I ended up going into the church, and sitting talking to myself, and maybe God. I had no idea what to do with myself. I was so, so sad.

9 December 2011

From the Eating Disorder Service, NHS

Dear Miss Davies,

We have received a referral from Dr ****** *******,
Consultant Psychiatrist, at the Eating Disorder
Service in Newcastle. As confirmed on the phone this
morning, I am writing with the following triage
assessment appointment:

Monday 12 December 2011 at 9 a.m.
With ******* ****, Senior Dietitian

Please do not hesitate to contact me if you have any
questions about the appointment.

Yours sincerely,

****** ****

Medical Secretary
On behalf of the Eating Disorder Service

Lydia Davies

After my diagnosis I was in complete denial. I was so detached from reality that I could not differentiate between dreams and real-life events. I was clueless as to which was which.

15 December 2011

A note left for my mum

hi MUM

I have had such a positive day for myself today. I enjoyed most of the falafel starters + stuff.

Then had a good SLOW supper INCLUDING carbs! + a second bit (small + early so don't worry) of spag bol.

I look forward to all the fun stuff we can do together when I am better.

I love u very much + see you tomorrow.

Lydia xo

From this point on I used my phone notes religiously to record my thoughts and feelings, as well as many crazy ideas and dreams that I had. I felt enlightened. I was running on a mixture of adrenalin, starvation and nervous energy. Combined, these fuels made me feel alert, invincible, powerful and generally wired.

I felt euphoric, as though I could achieve anything I wanted, and that I had the power to defy nature and survive on nothing. I wasn't like any other person around me; I had some special force within, to stay completely in control of my body. To me, everyone else seemed so bland, so conforming to the ideas of society. They woke up, ate, got on with their day-to-day tasks. I was always awake, never ate and had a mind spilling with important epiphanies, a special knowledge and outlook on life that no one else could even imagine. I did not need anything, sometimes not even water. I did not need people telling me I was sick. How did I know THEY weren't all sick? I was above all these people, floating in clouds and sparkles, on edge constantly, a beautiful nervousness and buzzing feeling that I could not describe.

21 December 2011

My blog post

Been looking at loads of inspiring stuff recently to keep myself on the right track:

- an old woman's M&S jacket that I ordered

- Bob Marley lyrics

- *Thin* by Grace Bowman

- the desire to pursue and achieve my goals

That book, *Thin*, is more comforting than I can possibly describe. Once I have finished reading it I will review it on here. (But I would already recommend it to anyone and everyone as it really gives such an honest and true account and deep insight of what this illness is like. It is the most accurate explanation and portrayal of the thoughts and ways it all works that I have come across . . . It's mad to read.)

But more inspiring than anything is the love and support I have received and am continuing to receive from my absolutely incredible family and friends. I cannot begin to explain how grateful I am for the people I have around me. I feel so lucky for being a part of my family, as each and every one of them is just

Lydia Davies

amazing. Their support inspires me. As does the support of my friends. Seeing some of the best the other night; although it was briefer than I would have liked, it inspired me and helped me gain further determination. I am eternally grateful for these people! XXO

28 December 2011

My blog post

<u>Christmas Day</u>

Woke up pure early, as per.

Did stockings in Mum and Dad's bed like babies.

Prepared carrots and sprouts like good daughter.

Drove to see the rest of the family in London. All of my dad's side of the family were there so it was quite a big one. We drank champagne and had high spirits. It was really nice for everyone to be there actually, as that's a fairly rare happening (especially as family live out in Cuba as well).

Then there was the lunch. A 20lb turkey (which still looked *huuuuuge* by the end of the meal; they will be munching turkey for weeks!). I feasted on my own lunch but developed a taste for parsnips and decided they are genuinely amazing. Felt like a bit of a turning point actually. Very positive.

Nap time/phone call time.

Present time – some money, which I plan to spend on some kind of magazine subscription . . . (otherwise I will just waste it on unnecessary items).

Drink more champagne and wine/be exhausted/want to get home/hurry up, Mum.

Home and MULLED WINE. Too much mulled wine actually, but it's so divine.

SO. In conclusion I had an amazing Christmas this year. I look forward to next year when I can maybe skip the nap part, and enjoy and indulge on even more parsnips – and perhaps other items too. Everybody overdoes it on Christmas Day. So it made me feel a lot better . . . everyone should be and is allowed to do so. Accepting that it's not wrong to indulge sometimes was a pretty powerful thought, I reckon. I hope everyone else had very neat Christmases and enjoyed their presents and parsnips as much as I did.

Peace out.

I felt very left out, which prompted me to make a very DRASTIC decision ... I was going to try a parsnip. I picked one out of the bowl in the middle of the table and dropped it in to my Tupperware, examining the coating of honey and oil as precisely as I possibly could. I took a tiny bite, and OH MY GOD IT WAS INCREDIBLE. I ate the whole holy parsnip piece, and proceeded to pile another eight onto my plate. I genuinely had never tasted anything so amazing in my life as the sacred honey-glazed parsnip. I ate more and more of them, my family

staring at me in both amazement and shock. I then asked for more and my father suggested that I might have had enough and should probably stop. I flew into a silent fury, ran upstairs and cried my eyes out, humiliated. I rang my boyfriend in tears for comfort, and then fell asleep for three hours from exhaustion, missing the present opening. It is a horrible feeling to have everyone begging and pleading with you to eat more constantly, only to have those same people tell you to stop eating when you are finally discovering the pleasure in food. It was both an infuriating and embarrassing concept to me. I understand that they guessed how bad I would feel after consuming so much, and they were probably trying to spare me from the painful emotions that would undoubtedly follow; but I just didn't understand how they decided and assumed that they had the right to tell me NOT to eat after telling me to eat for so long! I was five fucking stone, for god's sake, and all I ate was a few damn parsnips. They were all over double what I weighed, and had been stuffing their greedy gobs all day with piles of fatty foods. HOW DARE THEY? I would class this parsnip incident as my first binge, and there were many more to follow.

29 December 2011

My blog post

Hours pass at a time as I drift between thought and sleep through the night.

30 December 2011

From the Eating Disorder Service, NHS

Dear Dr *******,

Re: Lydia Davies. DOB 04.08.1991.

Thank you for referring the above patient to the
Eating Disorder Service. Lydia was seen by me for
assessment on 12/12/11.

Presenting problem:
Lydia suffers with anorexia nervosa.

Past history:
Lydia describes the problem originating in
depression. She has also become vegan as a bet with
her brother at Easter 2010, and had started losing
weight due to the change in her diet. This got worse
in the summer after she was diagnosed with genital
warts and found the diagnosis and treatment
humiliating and felt unable to tell anyone about it.
She spent a lot of time alone over the summer and
said she spent too much time thinking, which made

things worse. Her weight had dropped from around
60kg at Easter in 2010 to 47kg in the summer of
2011. Since returning to university in September
her weight loss seems to have escalated and by the
beginning of December 2011 she was 37kg. She is
aware that others think this is a problem and she
is very underweight, but Lydia's understanding of
how serious this is appears to fluctuate somewhat.

Current eating pattern:
At assessment Lydia described following a vegan
diet and avoids wheat as she believes she may be
wheat intolerant. She doesn't eat nuts as she doesn't
like them and tends to avoid carbohydrates.

A typical day's diet would be:
Breakfast – two spoons of oats
Lunch – salad with beans or tofu
Dinner – soup with salad and some kidney beans

   In addition, she drinks 1 litre of chocolate soya
milk daily and copious amounts of diet cola, tea and
coffee.

Weight and weight history:
Weight on assessment was 37kg, height 1.677m,
BMI 13.1.
   She said her normal weight has been around 60kg,
which would be a BMI of 21.

Bulimic behaviours:
Lydia said she had vomited on a few occasions in September when she felt out of control but has never binged and has not vomited for some time.

Cognitions:
Lydia described being unhappy with her body as she knew she was too thin.

Co-morbidity/risk factors:
Lydia feels she has suffered with low mood off and on for some time. She was prescribed Citalopram for this, which she found helpful, but this was stopped due to possible cardiac side effects. She said she sometimes felt quite low but would not do anything to harm herself.

Menstrual history:
Her periods started around age 15 and were regular until September 2010 when they stopped.

Family situation:
Lydia has moved back home to live with her parents. Her mother Beverley is 53 and is a yoga and sports teacher. Her father Mark is 54 and is a property broker who works abroad during the week and spends the weekends with his family. She has a brother, Matthew, 23, who is living at home and works as a music producer, and a sister, Pascale, who is 17 and at boarding school in Eastbourne.

Lydia Davies

Diagnosis:
Anorexia nervosa.

Summary:
Lydia is a 20-year-old student of fashion communication at university in Newcastle. She has had difficulties with low mood for some time and has been losing weight since Easter 2010. Her weight loss has escalated in the last few months and she has returned home to live with her family. She has arranged to defer her final year at Newcastle in order to concentrate on recovery from her anorexia.

She has been seen weekly at our service and has struggled to make any significant changes to her eating as yet. She has agreed to a referral being made to our day patient unit and if she has not been able to start gaining weight over the next three weeks would agree to start attending the day unit for refeeding.

She has also been seeing a psychologist privately who she said she found helpful and has been helping her to remain mindful about her difficulties.

Yours sincerely,

******* ****

Clinical Specialist Dietitian

2 January 2012

My blog post

New Year's Eve. New Year's Day. New Year's Resolutions.
New Year's Me. New Year's Eve was very neat. Lots and lots
of prosecco with a few of my closest friends.

Candle-lit dinner and nibbles with sparkling wine with some
relaxing company was divine, before heading down to a chilled-
out pub in Reigate for champagne and fireworks on TV.

I managed to stay out till midnight, which was an achievement
in itself, before heading home with my brother and friend to
watch *Bridesmaids* (again) and drink even more (prosecco,
Pimm's, finishing with mulled wine. ERROR).

New Year's Day, I'm pretty sure I was still drunk till at least
3 p.m. I felt fucking horrendous. So yesterday doesn't count.
My new year begins today and here are my resolutions:

–   First and foremost, recover. If you don't have your health
    you can't do a lot

–   French – an hour a day

–   Drink less alcohol

- Secure internship as something to work towards

- Be able to drive by Easter

- Be able to work and start a course by Easter

- Blog more frequently

- Drink fewer fizzy drinks

- Chew less gum

- Take an interesting photograph each day

Right, admittedly I've already broken most of these. But as general targets I hope they will help and encourage me to get better and make this year not like the last one. I hope to be where I want to be this time next year, and in order to do that I know what I have to do.

2011 happened in rapid slow motion. A turbulent experience that was so fast and involved so many events and different emotions that it felt equivalent to years. 2012 happened in just slow motion. The road to recovery is time consuming, difficult and exhausting. It is a dull process in comparison to the excitement and thrill that the opposite route I was previously endeavouring to take gave me.

6 January 2012

My blog post

Right.

I can't do this any more. I've gained a new level of determination now and I will not let it get away.

I will move to Paris. I will have a future. There are too many amazing people, goals, opportunities and ideas to waste. I've regained the desire to enable and give myself the chance to be able to explore the world and experience life.

Short, unexplained but necessary post.

14 January 2012

My blog post

THE ONE

Yesterday (yes, after a glass of prosecco – *in vino veritas*; I have become a strong believer of this, especially of the sparkling type), after a very negative and schizy few days, I had a positive change of mindset, which I am praying is THE ONE. It certainly feels like it could well be. I've even decided I like ketchup (not Heinz – you wanna get 'Real Ketchup', it's Unreal, trust). Anyways, I followed this positivity on today, ensuring I'd maintain this mindful state I have re-entered. The fact that I still have it today and plan to continue to do so is too good, and extremely vital when time is of the essence. Which I know now it very much is (and especially seeing as it's 2012 'n' that now, ha). I went to Brighton today.

I appreciated and was so inspired by the colours, sounds, people, clothes, and the general atmosphere (although I was absolutely freezing, etc.). It is one of the places I have always loved the most and feel at home at. Getting a little flat there and working in a vegan shop is yet another thing I would love to do.

Raw

Found some cool little pubs and vintage shops I'd not experienced before either, which I will definitely be returning to in the near future. I got a tattoo on my wrist at some place called Angelic Hell. The power I experienced from choosing something that I (as in the real me) wanted to do was an amazing feeling. It further enforced the FACT that I can turn all this around. If I focus on fact over feeling it is me that can do it. The pain of the tattoo across my bone was such a different type of pain from the kind I have experienced over this past year. It was inspiring, actually. I enjoyed the sense that it was a pain for a decision that I (Lydia) was making. Knowing it was a confirmed decision of something that I actually wanted to do to myself, rather than the act of something else causing / & that has caused me so much damage was just such a positive.

Meaning: I want peace with myself. The two arguing mindsets at war must find peace . . . and in order for that to happen I must remain mindful and push towards the necessary change. Every time I see it I will remember I must be mindful, and in the future when I see it I can reflect just how important and amazing to my life it was to make that peace. Lastly, I'm dedicating this long, rambling post that I'm sure many will not follow, to my brother. Thank you, brother, cos although you might not realise it you have helped and inspired me a ridiculous amount; you're like a good vice. And I appreciate it and your free-spirited self so much.

I love you xxo

17 January 2012

From my psychiatrist

Dear Lydia,

I received a letter from Ms **** from the Eating Disorder Service on 10 January 2012 informing me that you have decided to defer your studies and concentrate on recovering from anorexia nervosa. I think you have made the right decision for you as it was clear that you struggled to make changes while you were still a student at Northumbria University. I am sure that with the support of your family and input from the local eating disorder service, you have a good chance of making a full recovery. I anticipate that they will be managing the clinical depression that you have developed at the same time, although it is difficult sometimes to treat this while the patient is of a low bodyweight.

Can I ask you therefore to email us to confirm that we can discharge you, for the time being, from follow-up by our service? When the time is nearer to your return to Newcastle I would be grateful if the Eating Disorder Service could contact us to alert us to this so we can arrange to have a review with myself

Raw

and a member of the local community mental health team to agree on a care plan that would meet your needs.

Best wishes for your good health.

Yours sincerely,

Dr ****** *******

Consultant Psychiatrist

18 January 2012

From the Eating Disorder Service, NHS

Dear Lydia,

You have been invited to attend the Eating Disorder Unit for further appointments. These appointments are to continue the preparation process to determine whether day care is currently best to suit your needs and whether you might benefit from it. If these sessions indicate that day care is not the appropriate treatment option at this time, further recommendations will be made.

Yours sincerely,

******* *****

Specialist Nurse Day Care
Eating Disorder Service

18 January 2012

From my psychiatrist

Dear Dr *********,

Diagnosis: Anorexia nervosa (restrictive sub-type)

Medication: Nil

Weight: 35.3kg

BMI: 12.6

Level of Medical Risk: High

I just wanted to update you on Lydia's progress since her referral to our service. You will have received details of the assessment carried out by ******* ****, senior dietitian, on 12 December 2011. I have met with Lydia twice now, the first time on 11 January 2012 and again on 16 January 2012. She is really struggling to make changes to her eating pattern and continues to insist on following a vegan, gluten-free diet. Physically she is very frail. She was just about able to do the SUSS test and struggled to get up from squatting, but did not lose her balance. Her temperature was 36.2°C though she was peripherally cool to touch with some redness of her fingers, but no edema. She had an enlarged appearance of her parotid glands bilaterally and was chewing gum vigorously.

I understand that she has been seeing a private psychologist, **** ****** at Dorking, for CBT on and off since last summer and she reports finding this helpful. Unfortunately, however, her weight is continuing to slip down without evidence of stabilisation at all. I have spoken with her about the various options, including:

1) Her attending day care.
2) Her being referred for voluntary inpatient admission.
3) Her being referred for admission as an involuntary patient under a section of the Mental Health Act.

She was not keen on any of these options and insists that she is able to improve her health herself, despite evidence of the last few months being to the contrary. Lydia allowed her mother to join us at our last appointment. Mum expressed a significant level of concern about her daughter's state of health. Mother reports finding it difficult to support Lydia to eat as Lydia refuses to eat what her mother makes, even if it is gluten-free and vegan. Mum is surprised at the level of continued weight loss, though she did go on to disclose that Lydia had gone to Brighton on a train at the weekend to get a tattoo, and increased activity may have contributed to the weight loss. Mum also expressed concern about Lydia's drinking – she is drinking a glass of wine at night – and also her level of smoking – Lydia has picked up the habit of smoking and has told her mother that she can only eat if she is allowed to have a cigarette afterwards.

Following further discussion about the options open to Lydia, she is amenable to attending day care preparation appointments, though she believes that she is going to be able to stabilise her weight loss and show that she can gain weight as an outpatient over the next two weeks, and that actual admission for day care will therefore not be necessary. She is aware that if she is unable to halt the weight loss, then the level of medical risk may be such that inpatient hospital admission is unavoidable.

I will keep you informed of her progress.

Yours sincerely,

Dr ****** ***

Consultant Psychiatrist

This was the copy of the letter I received following one of my worst appointments. I was so delicate that I was barely able to walk. A healthy BMI is between 20 and 25, 18 and below is considered underweight, 16 and below prompts diagnosis of anorexia. Mine was just 12. A MCBT therapist told me that the lowest BMI he had ever worked with was 16 (which is still way under healthy). I was in an extremely dangerous place, and death was a definite risk. My heart could just stop pumping at any minute, and though I was aware of this it really didn't scare me. At this particular appointment, I should have been sectioned under the Mental Health Act. I have always been extremely persuasive, even as a child, and somehow managed to wangle my way out of it, promising that I would improve and that hospitalisation was not an option. Mother was distraught at the thought of me being sectioned . . . It stays with you forever, compromising future career opportunities, and preventing you from travelling freely to places like America. I was outraged that they thought I was mad. I was much cleverer than all of them put together. They were all older than me, but I had seen and experienced so much that I believed I had a higher knowledge of the world. I could see things in different ways to everyone, in ways that I could not explain and they would not be able to understand even if they tried. They were stupid, and I hated them for classing me as 'psychotic'. This is a word that was often used to describe me when I was attempting to explain my logical theories to the Eating Disorders Unit. Maybe they were just idiots and couldn't understand me because my level of intelligence and perception was miles above theirs. To be accused of being mad is something else. To be told you are going to die is okay, if the facts add up and the sum is realistic. But to be told you are mad? How can you measure madness? Everyone is different, and everyone thinks differently, therefore I find judging madness a little like judging art. My mind was an abstract work of art, a collage of colours and ideas. Their minds were like textbooks – boring, structured and unimaginative. In the car home after this appointment, my mother cried silent tears and I stared out of the window blankly. I didn't want to see her cry, especially not because of me. Halfway home the song 'Up' by James Morrison came on the radio. It was pouring with rain and we were driving down the gloomy motorway. The lyrics of the song hit both of us, and we both knew it. The song to this day means so much to both my mother and me.

Lydia Davies

CBT notes

* I feel fat = A FEELING. NOT FACT.

* I am fat = A THOUGHT. NOT FACT.

I weigh 34kg today = FACT.

I require a weight of at least 52kg to be
just normal = FACT.

I have not been able to sustain my weight gain = FACT.

I need professional help – day care = FACT.

18 January 2012

My blog post

Hello LIFE.

Each day could be a last day.

Fuck it.

Should be able to spend every single one the way I want to.
Last night I went to see *War Horse*. Was it good? I do not know.
Throughout the film so many things were concluded in my mind
and I had an amazing epiphany. Like, as in I actually had to
leave the cinema and go stand outside for five minutes just,
like, smiling and trying not to faint. It was euphoric. Wasn't sure
whether or not to be this open on tumblr. But like I just said up
there, Fuck it! Here are some of the things I wrote on my phone
during the film . . .

Reached the lowest point

At severe risk

That's been done now

You've done it now, now get better

Affecting about ten people in one night

Lydia Davies

For my parents

Do not want friends, friends of friends, friends' parents –
anyone – to need to worry

Upsetting everyone

Get better

Be determined

Get energy

Have life

Stop wasting precious time

Do it

Now let's live

Too much more to life than this

This post again may not make much sense. But I suppose it's
not really meant to. I know what I mean. I MEAN I'm going to
get better. I've flicked a switch in my head.

Tonight I am having curry.

Peace xo

20 January 2012

My blog post

Bit of a raw post but here goes . . .

It's 5.30 a.m. I'm walking round and round the house, feeling very anxious. I've been awake for the past three hours. Worrying about breakfast. Not even that I'm going to struggle really, more I just don't want it.

Just looked through my mum's diary of the weeks and weeks and weeks ahead I'm gonna have at home doing nothing but focusing on this. And the amount of appointments, ergh. Fuck that, I should be at uni having fun. I wish this had never happened to me and my life hadn't been taken over. It's been two fucking days so far and it genuinely feels like it's been two weeks' worth of munching. Cos it's so tiring physically and mentally. Like choosing what to have, when to have it, the anxiety of whether it's the right decision, the decision-making itself (I've always been ridiculously indecisive), what's normal, what will stabilise, what will gain, how fast will it gain. When will my legs not feel so weak any more, when will I experience hunger again? It's all such a time-consuming process. That's why I'm so sad it's happened; because now I want to be better . . . getting better is going to take as much time, if not more, as getting this ill did.

I suppose the only thing to do is use this sadness as determination. No relapsing. Cos that'll take away more of my life than has already been snatched away.

Why isn't *Neighbours* on at 7 a.m.? I would not MIND an episode.

21 January 2012

My blog post

A heart rock my mum gave me yesterday. She said she got
it for me because she loves me, and wants me to have a nice,
strong, red, healthy heart again as soon as possible. Ha ha.

Need to thank some people. All of the support I have been
receiving has been incredible, and I could not be more grateful.
Every message I receive means so much, and I am so thankful
I have such ridiculously understanding people in my life.

I've got to get better so I can give something back.

Pretty bland post but I'm feeling very low in energy from being
so overwhelmed with anxiety the past few days/nights. The
thoughts are so energy consuming it's ridiculous. For example,
spending several hours of precious sleep time schizing whether
it will be easier to have breakfast in pyjamas, or whether
I should get dressed first. Reading that, it sounds fucking stupid.
Ha ha. It's far too evaluating. I need to be mindful. Trying to
focus on the good is also exhausting. But it's a vital element to
all this. I am the biggest pessimist, so being positive is extra
tiring. But it will be extra worth it when I have life again. Cloudy,
cloudy post, but today I've got a cloudy head.

21 January 2012

Email from a friend

Hey Lydia,

I was just with my cousin and she mentioned that you're
not coming back to uni, and I wanted to just send you a wee
mail to say that I'm sorry you won't be back, but I'm glad that
you are hopefully getting better and just taking some time
at home! Don't want this to come across like I'm speaking
out of turn or anything. But I just wanted to let you know that
I have been thinking about you and I really hope everything
goes well for you, and good luck with all you do. Anyway.
Take care. Hopefully speak again in the near future!

Love,

R xxx

21 January 2012

Email from a friend

Hey Lydia,

Hope you had a lovely Christmas . . . Heard you're not coming back this semester. So sorry to hear that, hun; how are you getting on? I hope you get better as quickly as possible so we can see you again soon, babe! X x x x

24 January 2012

Email from a friend

Hey Lydia,
I know this is a bit random but I just thought I'd say I hope you get well soon xxx

27 January 2012

My blog post

I want my life back I want my life back I want my life back
I want my life back I want my life back I want my life back I want
my life back I want my life back I want my life back.

I've had everything snatched away from me and now I want
it back.

My degree

My graduation

My final year at uni

My friends

My independence

Any form of freedom

My ability to concentrate

My driving licence

Happiness

Fertility

Raw

Energy

Relationships

Family

Time

Lifespan

Motivation

Everything

Taken. Over.

FUCK IT. FUCKING FUCKING FUCKING SICK OF IT.

Going to be better. Want it all back.

I love you sister. Xxo

29 January 2012

My blog post

Uninspired?

I've been significantly less inspired during this week. Days can seem like years. 'Focusing on getting better' could not make things more confusing if it tried. Mind fuck. When stuck at home 24/7 there is no satisfaction from doing anything.

29 January 2012

Email from a friend

Hey Lydia!

Just wanted to send you a quick message to wish you all
the best with getting well again. I've been reading your blog
and I think you're doing amazingly! You're such a good
person; I know you'll be fine in no time. Take care, darling.
Sending love and good wishes xxxx

30 January 2012

My blog post

The dietitian

I hate this woman – like, I absolutely hate her. I'm pretty easy going, and open minded to everyone. Though I'd say I am quite a good judge of character, I'd never judge anyone before I knew them. Because that is just closed-minded.

Hate is a very strong word. And I can honestly say there is nobody else I know that I actually hate. This woman, however. This condescending, evil bitch of a woman. The way everything she says, she does it in an irritating, patronising whisper, staring pitifully at me as if I am about to die. The way she nods as if she's taking in what I'm saying, while she's looking me up and down as I speak (again, looking like she's about to burst into tears). The way she fucking makes me sit there for an hour and gives not one ounce of encouragement for the progress I feel I have made, but instead asks why I am chewing gum. WHY THE FUCK NOT? LIKE, WHAT THE FUCK? I am 20 years of age; I'm allowed to chew some gum if I want to. WHY DO YOU WEAR PURPLE EEEEEVERY TIME I FUCKING SEE YOU?? (Occasionally teal). (I did say this to her. She didn't like it. She went bright red. And patronisingly whispered, 'That's not relevant now, Lydia, really, is it?' followed by the nod and the sad expression.) Er . . . well, neither is the fact that I've got a piece of gum in my mouth. Who would want to spend 20 minutes talking about that? What a waste of my time.

She also undoes every single thing I say. Tells me I am in a psychotic state and that nothing I say when I am talking about why I want to get better makes any sense. WHEN IT DOES. She snatches my inspiration from me every time I see her and makes me feel completely rubbish and unmotivated.

Next time I see her I will say to her, 'You are the least encouraging and the most patronising beast of a woman I have ever met. The only ounce of inspiration I gained from you and your sessions was to get stronger so that I could ATTACK YOU. And burn your hideous purple attire.'

I was too close to saying this today but there was a medical student sat in my appointment. So although I was still fairly rude to her, I thought I'd save this for next time . . .

I HAD BETTER GET STRONGER FOR THEN.

31 January 2012

Email from a friend

Hey sweetie, the girls mentioned you aren't coming back
to uni. I really hope you get better soon and I'll be thinking
of you, xxxxx

1 February 2012

A letter from me to my parents

Dear Mum and Dad,

I am so so, so, so, so sorry for all the stress I have put you under, and the worry I have put you through. You are the best parents anyone could ever wish for and it makes me sad to think what I have put you through. You deserve a lot better. You, Matthew and Pascale are the reason I managed to find the courage to seek help in the first place. I couldn't get better for myself. That wasn't an option. But for all of you I try my best to be as brave and strong as I can be every single day . . .

This is much more difficult than you will ever understand; but it is for all of you that I persevere.

Every day seems like the length of a year. I spend most of it thinking or crying (usually both). And every night is almost as long (waking up feeling sick with anxiety, and sweating so much I have to get changed). The best word to describe how I feel, I think, is 'humiliated'. It's embarrassing waking up sweating and having a big agony stomach and being 20 and feeling like a lazy worthless slob. It's humiliating living off your hard-earned money like this; it's humiliating crying like a big out-of-control baby, having to leave meals early, hurting my family, having a life as sad as mine has become.

I am writing this to you because I am trying desperately not to push you away. I've lost my life, some friends, a boyfriend, my graduation, my freedom, my drive. Sometimes I stand and look at myself and wonder how on earth I went from being 20 at uni to back at home living like when I was 12. It makes me feel stupid. Like a complete failure. I also wonder where the hell my life is going. I have lost all sense of worth. I don't have any ambitions. I don't know what I want at all. I don't really know who I am any more. I feel completely broken. I'm trying so hard to be fixed. And when I shout and scream I don't mean it. I'm just frustrated because I'm trying to be fixed for YOU, not for me. So when you get frustrated at me or try to help me it hurts because I am already trying my best just for you.

I'm terrified, anxious, depressed, lost, confused and more than anything heartbroken at the state of my life.

I am aware I've got a lot of issues and I am sad about this because I've never wanted to disappoint either of you.

Thank you for standing by me even though I've let you down so badly. And sorry about this stupid letter but you're all I've got left so I can't shut you out completely.

I love you so much and will never, ever be able to describe how sorry I am to you.

Lydia xo

9 February 2012

From the Eating Disorder Service, NHS

Dear Dr *******,

Thank you for your letter dated 4 February 2012, which Lydia hand delivered to me here at the Eating Disorder Service clinic. Lydia has given me permission to discuss her treatment in our service with you, and with her consent I will arrange for you to be copied into correspondence to her GP.

Lydia is a very ill young woman and given the severity of her anorexia and her very low BMI score our treatment approach would include the prioritisation of weight restoration over psychological therapy at the start of treatment. This is because in our experience people at a very low BMI and very low weight often lack the cognitive ability to make use of psychological therapy. It would also be my preference for Lydia to have all treatment for her eating disorder be delivered within one service in order to reduce the likelihood of splitting and also to ensure regular communication of risk and a multi-disciplinary approach to the treatment and management of Lydia's eating difficulties. Lydia can access psychological support and therapy from within our service, though currently she insists on continuing to see you privately and she apparently values quite highly the work you are doing together.

At her last review on 6 February 2012 Lydia made clear her wish to continue to try to improve her nutritional health as an outpatient and she has turned down the day care place that was offered to her. In my view she remains very disordered in her eating and her insistence on continuing with a vegan and gluten-free diet despite the obvious physical risks to her health does concern me and the team greatly.

Yours sincerely,

Dr ****** ***

Consultant Psychiatrist

25 February 2012

Email from a friend

Hi Lydia,

Just a little message to say that I hope you are enjoying your time at home and finding the strength to get better. I know it'll be hard at times but I know you're strong enough and determined to get through it.

Lots of love xxx

27 February 2012

My blog post

Desperately trying to remember what I like and what I don't like, what I want, what I've done, what I need, what I thought, what I think, who I am.

The restrictions on what I can and cannot do are not helpful. A detachment from a normal way of life is like a detachment from reality. It confuses the mind, which is dangerous; the management of this is the most difficult thing.

Sitting, thinking, watching, thinking, reading, thinking, watching, thinking, sitting, thinking, walking, thinking, watching, thinking, sleeping, thinking.

Before – during – after THINKING. Thinking to the point where I don't know what I am thinking about any more. And then thinking about that.

27 February 2012

To the Eating Disorder Service, NHS

Dear Dr *******,

Thank you for your letter of 9 February indicating your opinion on Lydia's condition and the plan of action for her.

I am aware of the severity of Lydia's anorexia and her low BMI score and it is for this reason I have from the onset strongly suggested to her to adhere to any treatment plan that you have prescribed for her. However, it seems to me that the prioritisation of weight restoration on a voluntary basis over psychological therapy is proving to be rather difficult at the present moment. I believe that Lydia has insight into her condition and her cognitive ability is intact despite her maladaptive core belief, 'I don't want to be fat.' In my view it is this belief that is interfering with the recommended treatment plan. This is also compounded by her low self-esteem, anxiety, frustration and low moods, which I am helping her to address through various cognitive and behavioural interventions.

Over the past six weeks she has shown some degree

of slow but steady progress, which has resulted in some cognitive change and some weight gain. When she was weighed at your clinic in the second week of January 2012 she recorded a weight of 34kg and this has gone up to 40kg last week, according to her. Given this progress she told me that she is very unhappy to discontinue the sessions with me and I agree that it would only exasperate her feelings of anxiety and depressive symptoms. Her nutritional habits are still far from adequate and her vegan and gluten-free diet is also a concern to me but she is adamant to continue with it.

I entirely agree and support your treatment plan for Lydia and will continue to encourage her to adhere to it. In line with the multi-disciplinary approach to Lydia's managed care you have outlined I am happy to attend any reviews concerning Lydia's care if I get adequate notice and if it doesn't coincide with my clinics on Wednesdays and Fridays. Please contact me if you have any queries, preferably by email if you require a speedy response.

With regards,

Yours sincerely,

**** ******

Cognitive Behavioural Psychotherapist

16 March 2012

My blog post

This time last year I was preeeeetty happy. Things were neater. I was (slightly more) normal. I was caned constantly. I lived with some of the sickest people, I was about to go to Cuba, life was all in all NICE. My room was top, I was constantly rolling jays and watching all the seasons of *Weeds*. Uni was all right, pastimes were enjoyable, Starbucks was nice. So was Wagamama.

It is strange seeing how things can change so much within a year. The past few weeks have been a complete hell mentally. Every day feels the length of a year. Every time I'm doing something I'm thinking of the next thing. Life has been so uninspiring it's ridiculous. Isolation and recovery are fucking shit. It's all so opposite, it doesn't seem real. I'd like so much to be able to enjoy the things I used to enjoy, and see things the way I used to see them. My theory was 'we are atoms', as in we are just atoms, just a kabillionth of a pinprick in this universe, as in nothing really matters, everyone has problems. But think how massive the universe is in comparison to you and your issues. Trying to use this little theory to realise that there is life outside this fucked-up mental state. I know there is more.

16 March 2012

From the Eating Disorder Service, NHS

Dear Lydia,

I am pleased to now be able to offer you a psychology appointment with me. This appointment has been scheduled for:

Monday 23 April 2012 at 9.30 a.m.

This appointment will take place at the Eating Disorder Unit. The appointment will last for approximately one hour.

Yours sincerely,

Dr ******** ******

Chartered Clinical Psychologist

7 April 2012

My blog post

Completemindblock – picture = the epitome of how I feel.

Fairly over trying to seek out anything I find remotely inspiring to write about. It's not happening. Everything is so dull and so boring. Things I enjoyed before, bore me completely now. Trying to focus on small tasks that mean nothing just emphasises that horrible purposeless feeling. Trying to be positive only seems to make me more negative. Attempting something fun only becomes a massive chore. Every single thing I do I spend 90% of the time questioning why I am doing it. And coming to the exact same conclusion. I have no idea.

It was by this point that my affair with bulimia was getting more serious. What started out as just a little fun, gaining weight before my appointments to up my BMI, then fasting the rest of the week before repeating, soon turned into episodes of full-blown, uncontrollable eating and purging. I found more and more frequently that once I began to eat, I literally

couldn't stop. This was particularly prominent in the evenings, and after the consumption of alcohol. For someone who has been so strict with their self, and in control of every bite they put in their mouth, to going the opposite way entirely and not being able to stop it is an extremely frightening transfer to occur. I was assured by the EDS that the binging was purely a way of my body desperately attempting to get the nutrients it needed so badly, as I had deprived it for so long. It was like every time I ate, my body subconsciously thought this could be the last time in a long time it would be allowed food, so it went all out. I was promised and assured that this would stop once I was of a higher weight/BMI (lies). Before I could realise it, I would have consumed an insane amount of calories. Sometimes I would eat so much in one go that I genuinely could not remember what I had eaten. It was as if I was attempting to fill a bottomless pit, no matter how much I had, it was never ever enough. I could not fill myself up, there was always room for more. After an episode like this I would feel horrifically guilty and disgusted in myself. The next few hours would be spent downing pints of water and puking up my guts in a desperate attempt to rid myself of all the calories before they were absorbed. It was a race against time. I was painfully lonely. My days were spent in the house alone. My mother and father would go to work. I would watch my daytime TV, drink wine for lunch sometimes instead of food, if I was really bored. Which in turn would cause me to binge on roasted vegetables and things, before legging it to the toilet to try to purge as much as I could before my mother returned. I was talking to myself, depressed, and sat in my room in darkness, alone. There was no point in anything to me. I didn't even know why I was getting up in the morning. All I was going to do was watch TV and eat too much, and for what?! It was an extremely dark stage of my life and I have never felt more isolated or alone as I did then. I was also finding it very difficult to cope with the weight gain that the binging episodes were causing me. I was no longer doing it intentionally; I was an out of control mess, and a million miles away from my routine and controlled lifestyle that had been so accurately perfected.

12 April 2012

A letter from my sister

You need to GET HELP.

It has now got to the point where I am scared to walk into any room in the house. I'm scared to walk into the kitchen in case you start to scream abuse and throw things at me. I'm scared to walk into the bathroom as most of the time I am faced with vomit. And I am scared to go into your room as I'm worried one day I will find you dead. I don't know if last night was your way of punishing Mum, Dad and me but I cannot understand why you would do something like that at all.

I cannot live in a house which is constantly full of worry as to what state we will find you in next.

We have all been told that the only thing we can do to help is to love you. You make this extremely hard. We help and support you as much as we can, yet we still find notes telling us we are cunts and you fucking hate us. How am I supposed to love someone who can say those things?

That time when you went at me in the kitchen will always haunt me, as will last night. When you were

Lydia Davies

screaming at me I have never been so terrified in my life. I know Mum has had this before too.

You blame all of this on us but you're the only one that has the ability to change anything and make it better, yet you still refuse to get any help. None of us want to live like this and it is so frustrating as you are the only one with the power, yet something TRULY EVIL inside you is refusing.

All any of us want is for you to get better and be able to live a normal life and to be TRULY HAPPY, as you never will be if you can't accept that you can't do this alone, and it can't carry on!

I also wish you would stop talking about killing yourself. I have seen one of my closest friends go through losing his brother and I can't even imagine how awful it was and still is, not only for him, but his parents and also everyone he knew.

You have so much to live for but you need to reject the evil to fulfil yourself.

14 April 2012

My blog post

Parisparisparis

I had a very neat trip and am ever so grateful to my dad for taking me to Paris. I cannot wait to go back and enjoy the experience even more when all destructive and poisonous thoughts are eliminated. It will be too neat.

What I found most inspiring was: my dad's ability to be so patient with me and my irrational thinking. The quality time we were able to spend together in such an amazing city. The architecture, it's amazing. The lifestyle. How laid-back it is. How French it is. How fashionable it is. I just have to live there in a studio apartment with a pug called Almond.

15 April 2012

A letter from me to my parents

Dear Mum and Dad,

Yep, I've binged. So you can rejoice in secret that I'm not 'starving myself'. You have ruined my plan and my life, to be honest. I can picture you sitting and laughing at my uncontrollable binges together. Well done, you've ruined it for me.

I've lost uni, boyfriend, friends, everything in the past year. And now I've lost my figure too. I'm fat. Fat like you wanted. Well, it's disgusting. When I catch a glimpse of myself in a mirror (every two seconds at work) I wish I was in a balaclava and bin bag and no one could see my ugly self. I'm so disgusting I can't be me. I can't look at me. I just want to burst into tears all the time.

From tomorrow I am RAW. Don't bother putting negative spins on it and telling me I am 'ill' and will feel 'weak'.

No, I'm not ill, I'm just an extremely fat, greedy pig who has been tricked into believing greed is an illness. It's a fat girl. Lydia. Me. I will only be happy when I'm thinner otherwise I will take my life. I only want to lose half a stone. Stop taking all my fun with your lectures.

Stop putting that I 'starve myself' into my head.

Stop encouraging me.

Stop tempting me.

Leave me be.

Fat Lydia xo

For several months this is what my life consisted of. I was in a living hell, which I could not escape. No matter how hard I tried, I was well and truly stuck, and could not find an escape. I pencilled into my diary every time one of my friends was home from university, and I would be able to enjoy life briefly. I could not look in the mirror, showering was difficult as seeing my naked growing body disgusted me so much, I was constantly crying, deep in depression, trapped in my chaotic world.

16 April 2012

A letter from my dad

My darling Lydia,

I love you so much too and it makes me very sad to see you suffering so much. I wish I was better at helping you and I also wish I could get you the help you so obviously need; sometimes we can't do it all by ourselves and we need to find the right person/people to show us the way.

I do not want to lose you to this horrible sickness and I will do everything I can to help you break its grip so you can enjoy all that life has to offer again. You have family and friends, all of whom hope and pray we can get you back to the funny, lovely girl you were not so long ago, and still can be, I am sure.

Please do not give up, however hard things may seem. Your daddy and mummy need you. I have often told you the most painful and worst thing that could happen to me is to lose you to this illness.

I will do my best to keep strong for you and my family.

All my love,
Dad xo xo

17 April 2012

My blog post

Miss

I miss too many things

I miss all my friends

I miss being independent

I miss looking after other people

I miss set routines

I miss making my own decisions and choices

I miss being on a course

I miss having reasons to do things

I miss logical thinking

I miss last year

I miss old life

Nights like these are always skank. 3.33 a.m., wake up. Try to go back to sleep. Frantic thoughts. Mind racing. Regrets. Compromises. Anxiety. The xx's 'Heart Skipped a Beat'. Hot

Lydia Davies

water bottle. Binge. Read. More thoughts. What I wish I hadn't done. What I will do tomorrow morning. In each hour.

Too many things have been compromised. Too much time has been wasted. Too many people get hurt. I'd like to press pause at the same time as pressing fast-forward at the same time as pressing rewind. I'm claustrophobic.

If anybody actually reads these you must think I am genuinely mad. I'm not (well, I am, ha ha) but not a complete schiz (yet). XXO

The xx, Bon Iver, David Gray have disappointed me at this early hour and failed to work their magic. Back to trusty Coldplay it is.

20 April 2012

A letter from my sister

Lydia,

I wanted to write you this letter as I find it hard to express how I feel in any other way. I know you think you are okay and that we are all being ridiculous, but as far as I'm concerned, and anyone else is, you are far from it. I know it's hard for you to see something is wrong.

I even remember lying to myself and pretending everything was okay and normal, but this all really hit me that time when I came to visit you in Newcastle. You were getting changed and I just felt this huge lump in my throat as I had convinced myself everything was fine but it was one of the worst moments ever. When I got on the train after saying goodbye I instantly started to cry but tried to force myself to hold it in. Then I got in the car when Dad picked me up from the station and burst into tears. The harsh realisation of it all was overwhelming.

I know that it is so hard for you to see me upset, so I try to stay strong for you but sometimes I find it so hard to deal with. I also know that you can have the drive and goals so prominently one day but then non-existent the next.

Anorexia has completely changed you, which is not your fault. I have lost the Lydia that I loved spending time with, fighting over clothes with. I am adamant that you must get better so we can do the things sisters should do. I want to be able to go clubbing with you in London, go to Thorpe Park, go skiing, ice-skating – anything!

It's so difficult for you as you are constantly battling the voices in your head. Although you have reassured me not to be scared or worried, that is naturally impossible for me as your sister. There are so many possibilities of things that could be triggered by this disease and they are constantly on my mind. By writing this letter I am not trying to blame you for any of this or make you feel guilty . . . that is, in fact, the last thing I want to do.

I just want you to understand better how I am feeling as I find it difficult to express a lot of the time.

I love you so, so much that you don't understand and I just don't want to lose any more of my sister than I already have. I hope this can inspire you to an extent and help you realise that I believe you are strong enough to get through this. I have always thought you are beautiful but 'ana' has only made you change – and not for the better. I want my older sister back – to achieve this you have got to eat to function properly and to do all the things we miss doing together.

All my love,

Your baby sister,

Paskey xoxoxo

4 May 2012

My blog post

I find reality a mystery, a very difficult concept. The more days that pass, the less real life seems. I have even found myself questioning whether life is actually a dream and dreams are actually life. Some days I am convinced I am going to just wake up and all this time will have been a very long and detailed dream. I say detailed, however I genuinely cannot remember much since August. August–present is somewhat of a blur. Yes, I can remember elements of it but no detail, no feeling, nothing relevant. Each day I think might seem shorter ends up seeming never fucking ending! Tasks get set and goals get broken far too frequently. Each hour becomes too long. Focus is impossible. Concentration is non-existent. I haven't a clue what is going on and I fail to remember anything that happened in the past hour, let alone the past day/month/year. I'm not sure what is more ridiculous, myself, life or this blog post. Because NONE of them make any sense.

I have a strong feeling I should not post this because I sound genuinely mad. Fuck!

But really I could not give a fuck.

10 May 2012

My blog post

Refuse to admit defeat

I FEEL completely defeated. But I am NOT completely defeated. Feelings are not real. Facts are real. And it is a fact that so much bad is happening in this world, people suffering in countless different ways, people in the worst imaginable situations; my problems cannot be that big.

To me they can seem very big. Too big to face and to fight. But that would be so weak of me. Such a cop-out. If other people can get through this, and much worse things in life, then I can stop being such a pussy and deal with it. If there was a miracle cure I would take it in a second, but sadly there is not. Sadly it is all down to very, very, very hard work and perseverance. The support and attempted help I have received from those I love is incredible. I owe it to them to heal myself.

13 May 2012

My blog post

You know what?

Fuck them all. Fuck it.

VENOMOUS & ANGRY.

21 May 2012

My blog post

Never

Been this unmotivated

Or low.

Broken and can't be fixed.

Something or someone needs to get in my life and CHANGE it.

21 May 2012

A letter from me to my mum

Dear Mummy,

Sorry I am such a disgrace. I am a fat, greedy pig. It's disgusting. I am so embarrassed to be me, and I'm sure you are all equally (if not more) ashamed and disgusted by me.

The thought of going to work right now/anyone seeing me is making me feel sick. I have eaten a 'good lunch'. But it's made me feel even more greedy. This is not going to go away. I am not anorexic. I am greedy. I had control over it before, but now I have none. I hate myself so much. I don't feel content in any situation or place (apart from when I am asleep). I can't fit in anywhere. I don't feel happy or calm anywhere. I don't belong in this family, and it becomes more and more obvious to me all the time. I am not like you. I am not happy, kind or caring. Like ALL of you are. I'm selfish, greedy and embarrassing. I want more than anything to end it all, but I don't think I can because of what it might do to you.

Please, though. No more mention that I'm 'ill'.

Lydia Davies

I'm not. And the constant labelling of me as ill just
gives me some kind of excuse to carry on my
unacceptable behaviour. Which isn't what I want.
I am going back to raw veganism. My choice. I need
some guidance from something. I'm terrified of life.
I'm scared no one will ever love me again. This makes
me cry every night. I'm constantly scared I embarrass
and disappoint you. I'm scared I will never be
confident again. Or thin again. I don't know how
I will ever get a career. I worry that I can't keep my
room tidy. And that I watch time constantly. Basically
I really just don't like living. And I'm sorry for
everything.

But I just BEG of you. No more talk of illness.
I can see the fat on me. I can see what my scales say.
Don't try to tell me I'm not fat. I'm huge. The
number on the scale says it. I know what it says.
So don't try to convince me otherwise. Please!

Sorry I'm your daughter. Not the daughter you
probably wanted!

Love from Lydia xo

P.S. I cleaned your toilet. Sorry again. :(

21 May 2012

Email from a friend

Hiya Lydia,

Just seen a few of your posts on here and you seem really low; just wanted to send you a little message. At least on here you can either choose to delete or read anything and not have to listen to someone just talk at you. Want to urge you to keep your chin up and look back to your positive posts and artwork. When you feel dead shit and down remember what made you feel happy. Things are always gonna get rough but things get completely amazing too. You're a cool girl with loads of talent and a cheeky personality which will take you far. There's nothing not to like about you, Lydia; you're sound as fuck, funny and got bags of style. You may be feeling rubbish at the moment when it'll seem like your mates are finishing what you began with them and moving on to new and exciting things, but believe me, it's not too late for you to do the same. Look at me: closer to 30 than 21 and I've almost finished a course I don't want to do. So, fuck! I can do what I want, and so can you! Why not?! No one can ever say they've got or have done what they really completely want to do but you need to be happy

Lydia Davies

with the good things you've got; really good things, like your family!

I don't want to sound like a patronising preacher and you can tell me to fuck off if you like, but I just wanted to let you know, cos people don't tell the truth often enough or their feelings when they should be said.

If you need someone just to listen or owt, give me a bell, pet . . .

****

X X

23 May 2012

My blog post

Shit read

As a child:
I was extremely carefree, had a croaky voice and loved hugs.

My fondest memory:
There are too many. Water fight in the garden in Germany. France with Liv. Every special time with every special person. Laughing uncontrollably at the theatre with Jess. Being in the windmill.
   Travelling with the family. Just, loads.

I am not jealous of:
People who work hard to earn what they have.

I believe:
That we are atoms.

The last time I cried:
Yesterday. My bad.

If I could change one thing:
It would be my personality. I would make it not addictive.

Lydia Davies

The nicest thing:
Is being in Paris with my dada.

The shittest thing:
Is being stuck. Having nothing to do. Being let down. (And war.)

To me the word 'feminist' means:
Vote.

The last time I felt truly happy:
Was in Cuba.

In ten years' time:
I hope to look back at the current situation and laugh (even though it's not funny, ha ha). To be successful. Wouldn't mind a mansion as well.

My favourite meal of the day is:
—

When I was younger:
I wanted to peg up people's clothes for a living.

My favourite night in:
Must always include wine.

My simplest pleasure:
Is adding elderflower and a slice of cucumber to an icy cold glass of wine. Beautiful.

Getting old:
Is absolutely terrifying.

Raw

I could not get through the day:
Without nicotine or caffeine.

When I look in the mirror:
I try not to look in the mirror.

The biggest influence on the way I dress:
My mood. And cover-up, of course.

On my bedside table:
Are books that I don't read but make me look clever. Water, always water.

The person I spend most time with:
Is my mother.

The strangest thing:
Is the human race. We are so fucking weird when you think about it.

To me depression means:
Shit days, shit thoughts.

I've never had a crush on:
Anyone – cos I refuse to associate myself with that cringe phrase.

To escape:
I sleep. Failing that, I play Jetman on my phone.

I would like to say sorry:
To so many people so many times.

Lydia Davies

I have attempted suicide on several occasions in this state of mind. Trying to purge and not being able to is possibly the most heartbreaking and disappointing thing I can experience. Sometimes it gets so bad and I get so frustrated with my stupid body not being able to puke that I feel I have no option but to go to another drastic level of punishing myself and hurting my fat body. I have drunk cleaning product in an attempt to induce vomiting (didn't work), I have overdosed three times – partly in an attempt to make myself sick, partly because I feel so bad about my actions that I actually want to be dead – I have cut my arms and slashed my wrists, I have bitten and scratched myself and tried to suffocate myself. I even tried to drive the car on its roof, for god's sake!

25 May 2012

From the Eating Disorder Service, NHS

Dear Dr *********,

I reviewed Lydia in the clinic today. This was
an urgent appointment arranged following contact
with Lydia's mother who was concerned about Lydia's
mood. Lydia has been really struggling with feelings
of self-loathing and hatred and this is being
exacerbated by the binge episodes she is experiencing.
She left a suicide note for her parents and was found
by her mother with a plastic bag over her head
recently, prompting her mother to get in touch. She
feels low all day, every day, and her concentration is
poor, as is her volition. She feels death would be a
good escape from the anorexic thoughts and from
facing the aftermath of feelings following a binge.
Lydia describes feeling quite low in mood without
being able to see a future. She feels powerless to
control the binge episodes and restricts the rest of the
time. She struggles with sticking to the diet plan and
feels her days are full of thinking about food. She is
not driving and this restricts where and what she can
do. She also has no structure to her day as many

Lydia Davies

activities she had organised she either lost interest in or they fell through. She is also sad about the fact that she has not completed her degree because of the anorexia and today would have been the last day of her course.

Yours sincerely,

Dr ****** ***

Consultant Psychiatrist

28 May 2012

From the Eating Disorder Service, NHS

Dear Dr *********,

At her appointment with me today, Lydia reported persistence of the low mood. She said that the suicidal thoughts have abated somewhat over the past few days but are recurring intermittently. She said that when she wrote the suicide note last week and was found by her mother attempting to asphyxiate herself she did wish to die. She attributed this to intense feelings of guilt relating to having consumed her mother's cereal as part of a binge episode. Lydia explained that for her this incident represented the ultimate loss of control and reinforced the felt sense of hopelessness; in particular that, as she perceives it, her life presently has no purpose and is the source of emotional upset for others. Consequently, and as Lydia found it difficult to identify any concrete protective factors, I discussed with her the possibility of a referral to the Home Treatment Team. Lydia declined the option of this support and was emphatic in asserting that she will not end her life and is willing to hold the optimism of trialling the planned intervention when I return from annual leave. Lydia also confirmed she has the contact details for the out of hours telephone crisis support line and can of course present at A&E if there is any sudden further deterioration in her mood state. Lydia said that if she is unable to independently instigate contact with any such emergency service her parents, with whom she lives, would be able to do so. She can, of course, also contact our service for additional support if required.

With regards to the pattern of her eating, Lydia reports her subjective experience is that this remains relatively chaotic. The pattern is primarily characterised by dietary restriction interspersed with an average of four episodes of binge eating per week. Each of these binge episodes presently remains followed by purging in the form of self-induced vomiting.

Lydia's weight at her psychology appointment today was 43.3kg, which with a height of 166.9cm gives a body mass index of 15.52.

Lydia reports no other impulsive features to her presentation and in particular, no recurrence of the previous isolated instance of cutting. It would be useful, however, if ******* ****, Senior Dietitian, who is presently meeting with Lydia, could kindly on a weekly basis further explore the current level of alcohol use with her.

Raw

Treatment:

Lydia was open in explaining to me that she chose to meet with me today as she felt her choices were limited to this outpatient appointment or the potential need to revisit the possibility of preparation for day care. She explained she cancelled her most recent appointment with Mr ****** as she was mindful that it is not good clinical practice for someone to be engaged in therapy with two different practitioners simultaneously.

When I asked Lydia about her current motivation to undertake treatment, she explained she would like support with managing the current depression and anxiety and would also like to overcome the binge episodes. I explained to Lydia that it is not possible to treat the binge eating in isolation from the other disordered eating behaviours, in particular the dietary restriction, and she was seemingly accepting of this. I explained, though, that when there are concerns regarding mood state and the maintenance of safety that a precursor to the active treatment of the eating disorder is often an intervention designed to build adaptive coping and increase emotional resilience. We discussed how such an intervention would include the development of emotion regulation skills, distress tolerance skills, interpersonal effectiveness and consolidation of the core mindfulness undertaken with Dr ******. Lydia

Lydia Davies

expressed interest in undertaking such an intervention.

With best wishes,

Yours sincerely,

Dr ******** ******

Although I was eating a lot more calories now, mainly in the form of binges, the voice in my head was stronger and more brutal than ever. There was a constant devil in my mind. I have never been bullied, but the bullying I was doing to myself was worse than any harsh comment anyone could say to me. I ripped my own self-esteem to shreds and had zero confidence. I was ashamed to be me, and I wanted desperately to wear a balaclava whenever I left the house so that no one would have to look at my hideous face, and I could hide my humiliation beneath it. I wrote diaries and notes to myself constantly. Well, actually I didn't, the voice did. Reading them back the majority are in the third person, talking TO me, instructing and insulting me. By eating again and gaining weight the illness was absolutely furious. Anorexia hissed violent and messed-up things to me constantly.

1 June 2012

A letter from me to my parents

Dear Mum and Dad,

Firstly, again I am more sorry than you will ever know. I don't mean for it to be like this, and seeing how sad and disappointed you are in me makes me feel awful. I love you all so much, and I know you say you love me too but I can see you don't like me (and I don't blame you). Thank you for all the things you do for me, and thank you for trying to help me. I know it's not fair at all, and if I could help the pain it causes you I would.

I don't deserve the kindness you try to give me, and I was blessed to be given such amazing parents (and family). I dislike myself more than anyone! So I know how you must feel.

I am sorry again. Hate that I spoil everything (and I know that I do).

Loads of love from,

Your Lydia

XXO

1 June 2012

My blog post

List of things I hate/fear:

- the NHS

- eyeballs

- paper-cutting your eyeballs

- veins, arteries, capillaries

- spiders, eight-legged freaks of nature!

- Being by myself

- Missing out

- The future

- The sea (and getting munched by a shark)

- Getting attacked

- Carbohydrates

- Stubbing my toe

- The dietitian

Raw

- Not getting to the car first on a dog walk
- Not being able to sleep
- Dairy
- Big horses
- Hospitals
- Flapping pigeons

31 July 2012

My blog post

The summer so far has been horrible and quite good. Driving
is also a massive positive. I feel proper powerful zooming around
with Above & Beyond at chav volume with the windows down.
It's my favourite thing to do. Though I am an absolutely awful
driver. But, but, but, this summer has been bad. Because finding
a job is impossible. Recovery is still like hell. My plan to transfer
uni ain't happenin'. I can't sleep. I get too easily bored. My room
is the messiest it's ever been (perhaps reflecting my head).
Everything just seems impossible, and like nothing is going to
work/happen/etc., etc. On top of that, I miss my uni friends, and
uni/having a focus, my last summer, the sun, having money,
blah, blah, blaaahhh.

3 August 2012

My blog post

This time last year was SO much better than this time this year. All I can hope is that this time next year is better again.

Peace & love. Xxo

The next big commotion in my life was extremely dramatic. I had been drinking wine at my friend's house. I had driven myself there and the plan was for me to stay the night. As we spoke and laughed in her kitchen together, into the late hours of the night, I became increasingly drunk. It was one of those situations where I was drinking for the sake of it, every time my glass became empty I felt empty, so I would top it up constantly. Molly likes a glass of wine, too, but that was the difference – she could enjoy just one glass slowly and feel content, while I downed glass after glass, feeling less and less content.

As it got later, and I got drunk, my appetite increased, and I could feel a binge coming on.

Generally speaking my binges only usually happen in the comfort of my own home, and there are only a handful of occasions where they have taken place either in other people's houses, or in public – on a train for instance. Once Molly went to bed, I could not stop eating. I bought myself some things to munch, but as soon as they were gone I needed more. I ended up eating a stupid amount of food out of Molly's family kitchen, and I am still so ashamed of myself to this day.

When the binge episode was over, I felt so humiliated about what I had done, and incredibly guilty for taking what wasn't mine, that I needed to get out. I could not be sick in her house; she has a little brother and it felt wrong and disrespectful to do so. In a state of complete embarrassment and dread about the consequences of my behaviour, I decided I had no option but to get out and drive home. As I sped along the road completely oblivious to how terribly and carelessly I was driving, I could barely see the road. My eyes were hazed over and the only thing I could see was the purge at the end of the tunnel. I was nearly home and swung round the bend of the dark country lane. I remember feeling like I was going too fast, I felt a little out of control, then I felt a lot out of control. I attempted to slam on the brakes when it hit me how fast I was going, and I don't know exactly what happened next, but I can guess I hit the accelerator rather than the brake. There was a heavy thud that vibrated right through me as the left wheel hit the bank along the side of the very narrow road. Next thing I knew I was flying through the sky and my mind was shouting, 'THIS IS IT THEN. THIS IS IT.' It happened scarily quickly. Spinning through the air upside down in my car was the craziest feeling – adrenalin pumped through my body, and thoughts screamed through my head. This changed in a split second when the car came smashing down upside down onto the road. I heard an almighty crash of the car landing, and the glass shattering into a million shards.

I woke up upside down in pitch-black silence. The first thought that came to my head was that I needed to get out of the car in case it exploded. I used my arm to smash away the remaining glass from the window, and crawled out. I could not believe what had just happened and was in shock. I ran away from the car screaming for my mum and dad. It was a good half-hour walk down dangerous country lanes to my house, but I was too scared to re-enter the car to find my phone in case of a fire or something else hitting it. I started jogging in the direction of home. The only sound was my screams for help and my parents. Tears flooded across my cold face as I ran as fast as I could, struggling to breathe and calling out for help the whole way. There was no one to hear my cries, though. I was alone and anything could have happened. As if that was not dangerous enough, I then proceeded to flag down the first car that passed. A man stopped, and I climbed into the back of his car, confused and desperate. Luckily he was not a serial killer and drove me home, where I got out and screamed for my mum and dad once more till they opened the door.

8 September 2012

My blog post

LIFE

My serious lack of appreciation of life came crashing down on me (literally) last night.

I have realised how numb I have become to living life. I have realised how trapped in my own head and thoughts I still am. There has to be more to life than living in fear and regret of every small decision and choice I make. And thinking and thinking and thinking and never stopping thinking and analysing every single thing I do or move I make. Down to the sound of the rhythm of my blinking and breathing. It's not fun. It's not living. It's not being alive. It's being trapped. Trapped. Dull. Bored. Stuck. Not moving. Static. Confused. Unappreciative. Ungrateful. Caught up. Closed off. Long. Watching time. Slow. Lazy. Unmotivated.

I believe an angel saved me last night. I know who she is. She protected and shielded me completely, which is quite a miracle. She followed above me as I ran home, until I was there safely (amazingly). I feel extremely undeserving of everything I have . . . including life. But perhaps there is more meaning, reason and purpose to my life than I can see. Perhaps that's why I was spared (again).

It should not take a near-death experience to scare someone into realising what they've got and how lucky they are. And it most definitely should not take three. In one year. It just shows me how dazed I am. Glazed over and uncaring about everything. I felt no real fear. My mind was elsewhere, as always. And I'm being honest when I say that. A couple of years ago if I had had the same experience I would have been so shaken up and affected by it I'd have been a complete wreck. But I am already such a wreck that there isn't much more wrecking that can take place.

Anyway, I have learned. I have the most amazing family and friends, for supporting me and understanding me and listening to me. Life cannot and should not be taken for granted. I have been given another chance so I must be so grateful. I have a guardian angel. I must start doing things that make me genuinely happy. I must re-learn fear. Appreciate life.

14 September 2012

My blog post

The good, the bad and the ugly

I'll start with the good . . .

I'M ALIVE

I have the best friends I could ever wish for

My family are amazing

I have a warm bed in a warm house

My life is extremely fortunate in many senses (and I must remember this)

I can see, hear and speak (maybe not feel, but I'm working on it)

The bad and the ugly . . .

I'm still not myself

2012 has been the worst year of my life, so far

I have lost a lot of things I worked so hard to get

I put pain, stress and pressure on the people I love the most (I'm sorry)

Lydia Davies

I cannot say sorry as many times as I want to

I cannot show I am sorry exactly how I want to

I have uncontrollable thoughts and my mind is impossible to switch off

I'm quite possibly mad

My consumption of alcohol had increased to the point where I was drinking every day. When I saw friends we would go to the pub, or drink wine at each other's houses. My new mechanism for dealing with my problems and the voices was to plaster them over with alcohol. This habit confused everyone, as alcohol has such a high calorie content, and I was happy to drink copious amounts of it. The difference between the calories in alcohol and food, though, was that alcohol made me feel different, drunk, and helped me forget; food, however, made me remember how fat and ugly I was, and always made me feel horrible after. These alcohol-infused nights usually ended in an almighty binge-and-purge session. Alcohol enhances sensations, including hunger. Nothing was more attractive to me than the thought of gorging on everything in the kitchen when drunk. The best part about it was that I was so drunk I didn't care or worry about what I was eating. Purging was also easier due to the amount of drink in my system. The worst part was the following day. If you have ever had a bad hangover, times that by ten and you have a food-over. Waking up with sick-splattered pyjamas, a hugely bloated stomach that resembled an 8-month pregnant woman, agony jaw, head, oesophagus, ulcers blistering the mouth and tongue, the most unquenchable thirst you can imagine, and a churning gut. All those feelings on top of a ghastly hangover equal an extremely painful and uncomfortable day; until it hits 6 p.m. and it's acceptable to drink again.

18 September 2012

A letter from me to my parents:

Dear Mum and Dad,

Firstly, sorry.

I have a disgusting confession. I wish I hadn't, but I did. I drank wine from the fridge. I am so sorry. I feel like a horrible thief. It wasn't mine. I shouldn't have done it. I couldn't just have one glass. Lost control. Then ate all the biscuits, all the butter, all the jam, all the bread. Chocolate. Yuck. I can't believe it. I can't stop. I didn't even want to eat. I had a good supper. I'm trying SO hard. I just feel helpless. Maybe I could start telling you what I want and I am not allowed to prepare my own food? I can't do this for much longer. As much as my mood has improved – how I really feel hasn't. My stomach is absolute agony on a daily basis because it's so bloated, stretched and full. I can't sleep because of it. This is due to binging, and I'm sure alcohol. My skin is lumpy and in rashes on my neck, stomach and back. I have headaches, feel sick and just lazy and shit.

Raw

I hope to God I don't wake up tomorrow because I know how unhappy I am going to be; it's unbearable. It's even harder trying to be happy when I'm really, really not.

Telling you today that I have a problem with drink was so shameful. I have let the whole family down now in every possible way. I hate myself. If I could switch lives with anyone, or just not be here any more, I would in a second.

I am SICK of this happening to me. I am sick of my life and myself. I am sick of upsetting the people I love. I am sick of being trapped in this absolutely disgusting body.

Tomorrow I am changing. I can't cope any more. I feel by myself (although you and everyone offer me so much support – thank you). But I feel I am stuck as myself. Going nowhere. Achieving nothing. Ruining everything. The physical and emotional pain are too much. I'm just desperate for it to end. But I am scared of the future, and don't know where I am going. Without a set aim I can't achieve anything. Ergh, I hate, hate, hate, hate, hate my repulsive greedy gluttonous self. Why can't I be as good as you/ the rest of the family?! I'm sorry I can't. I wish more than anything I could. I am a disgrace. A horrible, horrible beast. I've tried to take some tablets (not too many, so I'll be fine); hopefully I might just get a long sleep.

Probably don't talk to me/see me tomorrow

Lydia Davies

because I know how terrible and disgusted I will feel
when I wake up. I am scared to wake up because of
this.

I love you both so much xxo

9 October 2012

From the Eating Disorder Service, NHS

Dear Dr ***,

I understand that Lydia has not recently attended her appointments with our service and was consequently asked to contact us by 16/10/12 if she wished to receive any further support from us at this time.

You will be aware that when I last met with Lydia (01/08/12) for a psychology review appointment she reported a good level of coping. She described her mood as upbeat and reported no suicidal ideation and little emotional reactivity. She also denied any recent episodes of binge eating or purging and said that the self-harm was limited to the dietary restriction; in this respect, Lydia reported following a regular though highly restrictive eating pattern (no breakfast; beans, salad and soup for lunch and dinner; and a couple of glasses of wine most days).

At her psychology review appointment Lydia attributed the improvements in her mood, the disordered eating behaviours and weight to the pre-scribed antidepressant medication. She also explained that with such improvements she no longer felt there was a clear rationale for undertaking the planned psychological therapy; that is, in the context that the preliminary treatment goals she had identified were to improve her understanding and management of her emotional experiences and to overcome the binge eating. In this respect, Lydia understandably presently experiences the dietary restriction as egosyntonic; as such, whilst it was explained to her it is not possible to address the binge eating in isolation, she has consistently been open in expressing she is not presently motivated to address the dietary restriction. At her psychology review appointment Lydia expressed surety about her choice not to proceed with the planned intervention and declined to complete a decisional balance analysis.

At her psychology review appointment it was unclear whether the antidepressant medication was to some extent blunting Lydia's emotional experiences and therefore understandably reducing her motivation to engage in treatment. Alternatively, she might be continuing to experience high levels of emotional pain but feels for the present time unable to approach treatment and did not feel able to directly voice this. If the latter suggestion more accurately captures Lydia's current experience, I would be concerned about the continued risk she potentially represents to herself, particularly in the context of the previous, multi-impulsive features to her presentation; namely, the binge eating and purging, alcohol use and recent history of suicidal ideation and suicidal/para-suicidal behaviours. In this respect, I am pleased that Lydia has expressed some willingness to re-engage with our service. I also hope that through attending an appointment with ******* she will be able to further authentically discuss her current experience and any continued plan; namely, her dietetic appointments and outpatient psychiatric review appointments. I also anticipate that her appointments with ******* will support Lydia to consider how best to manage the risks represented by any residual behaviours, including ongoing arrangements for any required medical monitoring.

If further to re-engaging with our service Lydia wishes at any point to revisit the option of psychological therapy, I would, of course, be willing to meet with her to discuss this possibility further to a re-referral from you or ********.

It was a pleasure to albeit briefly work with Lydia and I hope to be able to be of assistance to her in the future if required.

With best wishes,

Yours sincerely,

Dr ******** ******

30 October 2012

A letter from me to my parents

Dear Mum and Dad,

Firstly, SORRY. I am so unbelievably sorry I have already made this past year absolute hell for you both. And this just tops it off really. I bet you never thought I'd turn out to be such a problematic child. I've always wanted to make you proud of me more than anything. And I know I have failed. I have been trying really hard but I know it's not good enough. Lately I have felt defeated and like I really don't belong in your home. My horribly out-of-control behaviour happens mainly here, and I hate that it's always you who get affected by it. You have been the best parents I could ever ask for and although I am hardly able to show it any more, I am so grateful. I am going to try so hard from now on to make your lives easier and happier. The way they should be. I have been taken over by all-consuming selfish thoughts which have contributed to the person I have become. Selfish, greedy and horrible. I want to be selfless, giving and kind, though, more than anything. Especially to you because you have put up with so much of my shit.

Raw

I am going to help more around the house. Not answer back or shout and try my hardest to resist the temptation of bingeing and purging. I am going to save money and pay you back for the car (in instalments) and put my determination into making all our lives better, by setting goals and working to achieve them.

I can't tell you how sorry I am or how much I love you because it is so much.

Lydia xo

2 November 2012

From the Eating Disorder Service, NHS

Dear Dr ******,

I reviewed Lydia in clinic on 22 October 2012 with
******* **** (Senior Dietitian). Lydia had not been
seen at the EDS since July 2012. She is maintaining
a slightly higher weight and reports her mood has
improved due to medication and having some work to
keep her occupied. She has requested discharge and
monitoring via her GP. Lydia declined to be weighed
but she appears to be a similar weight as at the last
weighing, which would be a BMI of 15–16. She
continues to restrict her intake, having a diet of
around 600–900 kcals per day of soups and salads.
She drinks some alcohol and binges on average twice
per week, after which she vomits. She continues to be
very concerned about weight and shape and the kcals
in the food she eats. Lydia's parents got in touch in
September to alert us about a RTA that Lydia was
involved in. She was staying at a friend's house and
binged on food from the kitchen. She had been
drinking and felt so guilty about what she had done
that she left the house and tried to drive her car

home but crashed it. The police breathalysed her but she was not found to be over the drink-drive limit, though she thinks she probably was. No further action is to be taken by the police on this matter.

Lydia feels her mood is better, which she believes is partly due to working most days in Monsoon in Reigate. She does not wish to continue being seen at our service and said she had started to see a cognitive hypnotherapist privately and thought this might be an interesting approach to getting help. She does not want to be monitored at our service but would be willing to be seen monthly at her GP's surgery to have bloods taken and for weight monitoring. She does not wish for us to arrange a discharge review at her GP's surgery, but requested we write a letter informing her GP of her discharge.

Yours sincerely,

Dr ****** ***

Consultant Psychiatrist

It was around Christmas 2012, and I felt so different than I had done the previous year. The glitter seemed dull, the lights were not so bright, the excitement was half-hearted, and I wasn't really looking forward to it, to be honest. I was

completely out of control with my eating and knew that this day of food was going to be one of the biggest struggles I had faced all year. I love the smell of Christmas food, and I could clearly remember how amazing the parsnips were the year before. What didn't help is that we had Christmas at home, and home is the place when I lose control the most. I feel on edge but too comfortable there. It is my habitat and it's as if no one sees me when I am behind the closed doors of my house. I turn into some kind of animal, all emotions are let loose, all inhibitions lost. I cannot walk into my own kitchen at home without considering a binge. I cannot walk into the bathroom after eating anything without considering a purge. I drank too much champagne (again) before Christmas lunch was served. I can't say I even remember it, but I know I ate way too much, and I remember sneaking in and out of the kitchen long into the afternoon, and then in and out of the bathroom trying to rid myself of the food I had not deserved. I hated that day, and felt selfishly envious once again of everyone else's enjoyment.

24 December 2012

My blog post

This time last year I wrote a blog about everything I love about Christmas.

This time this year I am going to be a depressing old toad and write a blog about everything I hate about Christmas . . .

Turkey. Chocolate. Meat. Meat. Meat. Gravy. Mince pies. Christmas pudding. Brandy butter. Cake. More chocolate. Food full stop. Bet no one even really likes turkey anyway.

Money. Biggest waste of money there ever was. Don't actually need half the things we give or get really.

Tradition. You have to be happy and smile at ALL times.

Small talk. 'Merry Christmas', 'Have an amazing Christmas' . . . Nah, it's just another day really, isn't it?

I could go on but I won't. Have an amazing Christmas anyway.

30 December 2012

My blog post

2012 has been an intense year. For a lot of people. I don't think I have learned much. I'm also not sure I've achieved much. Those closest to me may argue that I am in a much better place; however, I beg to differ as I've not got a clue! Instead of learning new information it feels more like I've forgotten lots this year. It's gone by so fast yet I've done fuck all, which is somewhat depressing to think about. I think I would rather forget 2012 ever happened . . .

By this time next year I hope to be writing a blog saying how fucking amazing the year has been, how much I've achieved, learned, seen, done, given. This will be a proactive one. I can feel it in my bones. Best wishes for the new year; make it what you want.

3 January 2013

A letter from me to my parents

Dear 'parents',

I am so sorry I am like I am. I am a fat, ugly beast and I know it. I just can't control myself any more. I don't know why I'm here. I pray every night that when I finally fall asleep I might not wake up. I know this may upset you, but it's the only thing that excites me.

I'm miserable. I'm living for nothing. I'm just existing. And fucking up things for other people. Especially all of you. I don't know how I got to be so sad, bored and lonely. But I am. I'm SO lonely. The only thing that makes me feel less alone is eating too much. And that's not me. It makes me more unhappy. And it makes you unhappy. I can't sleep in my room. I don't belong here. I sleep in the spare room because I'm a guest in this house. I'm not one of you. I don't belong here. I've never fitted in and never will. I feel constantly judged. I hate it. I hate being me. I hate 'Lydia Davies', whoever the fuck she is. I'm so ashamed of myself. I just don't want to be here. I don't want to see or speak to anyone any more. I'm so sorry you had me. That's the only thing I think you have ever done wrong. If you hadn't had me, imagine how great everything would be. I'm so sorry for burdening you. I'm fine and please put all your time into your other two great children. I've wasted enough of your time and energy already. I'm sick of my life. I'm sick of remembering all the things I've lost and worrying that I won't find them again. I hate all the food in this house. How much all of you eat. How I sit all day with nothing to think about but all the Waitrose stuff in the kitchen. About how I've failed. About how I lost the person I loved this time last year. I do NOT want to talk about it.

I do not know why I wrote all this (apart from to apologise for being here – again).

Fat. Hideous. Lydia hippo.

I strongly believe in NOT talking about people behind their back. Yes, I am extremely guilty of having done this, and probably unintentionally still am, as it is difficult to avoid (even in this book I am doing exactly that); it has become a part of our culture unfortunately. However, if this illness has taught me anything, it is that honesty most definitely is the best policy. I had every tiny bit of privacy confiscated from me, and had to readjust to being watched constantly,

and violated physically and mentally. The prodding of needles into my every vein to extract my blood which I did not offer, the digging around my head for answers and give-aways, the weekly documentation of my weight, heartbeat, feelings, thoughts and mood. When put in such a position there comes a point where there is no point in trying to keep everything a secret. You become so exposed that you may as well walk around naked shouting your most private secrets through a megaphone. It's strange to think about really. I used to be the most secretive person I know. I kept things to myself; I was embarrassed extremely easily, and loved the element of mystery that my character portrayed. To go from that to an open book of big blatant letters and words projecting out of me for all to see and read, is such a contradiction. It is as if through my self-destructive illness I lost all self-respect, self-control and morals towards myself. I used to care so much what people thought about me, and though I am still very self-conscious, it is more my own opinion of myself that matters, as I know everyone else who loves me excuses my barbaric behaviours, and puts them down to the fact that I am ill, rather than the fact that I am horribly out of control. Sometimes I find words spilling out of my mouth regarding very personal occurrences, ones that I would wish to keep to myself, but I cannot help but spew out this information before I realise that in fact it is pretty private. Once said I cannot take these things back, and the more I let out, the less privacy I have, and the less shame I feel.

10 January 2013

My blog post

I have no secrets.

I really don't. I seem not to care as much what people think any more, which causes me to say more than I mean to.

Back in the day I was a dark horse. Now I'm an open book.

This probably made no sense to anyone. Or it shared far too much, again.

11 January 2013

My blog post

'Everything's an illusion and nothing is real' is my favourite quote. It is from the Van Morrison song 'Enlightenment'. I don't think I am enlightened as such, far from it, in fact . . . I do, however, think I see things differently to the norm. My personality type is auditory digital. People of this type often have a constant conversation going on with themselves, attempting to find meaning and reason within things. (Save that for another blog.)

Walking down a short dark hallway (drunk and high) to the toilet, I suddenly have absolutely no idea who I am, and I feel really sad and lonely. When I get into the light I look at my face in the mirror and do not recognise myself. The person staring back at me could be anyone, someone I have never seen or met before. I don't know what I want or why I am me. Walking back down the dark hallway, the sudden wave of loss, insecurity and confusion hits me again. I am lost, I don't recognise anything. Someone bring me back, please. Help me. And I feel sick. There is a tangled knot in my stomach; a combination of emotion and food, my abdomen is swollen with both. The sadness wells up inside of me, and my eyes prick as they brim with tears of frustration, the realisation of the loss of my identity. I see this kitchen not as a place of family, feeding and nurture, but as cupboards packed with ingredients for recipes of disaster. The items stare me in the face, before leaping down my throat, brushing past my taste buds, and then spreading their evil across my body. My stomach is like a cauldron, swilling and brimming with a mix of rancid food and toxic emotions, creating a strong potion of self-hate. Where the fuck am I? If I close my eyes will I wake up in the middle of the ocean? I have wandered miles now, searching for myself. Ambling down dark and twisted pathways in the cold silence, hoping that I may bump into myself and we will be able to reconnect, become one again. I will get to be myself again and finally remember who I was; who I am. I can only remember sections of myself, things that upset me, things that made me laugh, things that I feared and things that I liked. But the cement that holds these bricks of memory together has worn away, disintegrated. Without this cement the foundations of myself and the structure of who I am are lost, and I am just a pile of rubble.

Lydia Davies

A mixture of emotions and memories scattered across the floor, some cracked, some strong, but missing the vital framework which seals them together.

18 January 2013

My blog post

Convinced I will go to sleep and wake up in a different time, place or world. Spiralling thoughts.

No idea where I am in life! Focusing on the future. Cannot forget the past. Trapped! Wrong place.

29 January 2013

My blog post

Feel like the bag of ski clothes in the attic. Just sitting there with no purpose all year. Hmmmmm.

11 February 2013

My blog post

I got accepted back to uni in Newcastle today. It will have been two tough years since I suspended my studies. It's proof to myself and everyone else just how far I've come. On my own. By myself. After refusing all that help. I achieved this.

17 February 2013

My blog post

The people I love are the only reason I kept going in very black times. They are the reason I bother to get up every day. They are the reason I've put up with a lot when all I've wanted to do is give up. As much as I want to be with these people for every moment possible, I want to go and be far away from them too. I think they need their time. I'm tired of causing sadness. I want them to be as happy as can be because they deserve nothing less.

22 February 2013

My blog post

Things I hate . . .

Being told what to do. I have always hated this. If I am going to do something I will do it for myself. There is no point in trying to instruct me, as it will only encourage me to do the complete opposite, unfortunately.

Since my diagnosis I had fantasised about going away, getting out of England, and more importantly getting out of my head. I strongly believed that I needed to see and experience other parts of the world in order to want to truly recover. I needed to see something other than my dull bedroom, the shop I worked in, or the bowl of the toilet. 'Inspiration and influence are key words' is from something I wrote in my phone at the start of my illness; 'creativity and drive will save me'. It was a bit of a Catch-22 situation. I needed to get better to go away, but I thought I needed to go away to get better. I saved up some money and booked a flight out to Hawaii in February 2013. Hawaii is an extremely spiritual island, situated miles away from other lands. I was invited to stay with my dad's friend, Rachel. Rachel and I had only met twice before I flew out to meet her; but she invited me and meant it, and I jumped at the chance as I felt deep down that it was something I needed to do.

27 February 2013

My blog post

Hawaii

I can tell you at home I spend the day craving the night so I can be asleep again.

It's so neat how being surrounded with such positive energy and genuinely happy people who love life changes your perspective and just lifts your spirit.

28 March 2013

My blog post

I am getting lots of great inspirational words from anonymous people. I like getting them and reading them, and what has been said is all very true and does make me think and remember how lucky I am. I used my blog to complain a lot. In real life I don't complain as much as I could – though I know I complain more than I should. So I'm liking all these positive comments. I am grateful for what I have . . .

. . . (but getting new shoes still does make me really happy).

18 April 2013

My blog post

This week in general has been pretty fucking shit. Apart from a bird taking a shit on my head (which I found extremely distressing), I have dyed my hair an unfortunate shade of bright yellow (genuinely cannot look in the mirror) and forgotten tablets on numerous occasions, which has made me anxious as fuck! And I have absolutely no money. I also had to return my beautiful Dalmatian shoes due to lack of funds, which was very upsetting. I have injured my knees from attempting to run cross-country in Reebok high-tops on a daily basis (idiot). WHAT ELSE? I feel like I've just been pissing everyone off because I mess so much stuff up. AND I'M SO GODDAMN FRUSTRATED AT MYSELF MORE THAN ANYTHING (APART FROM LIFE IN GENERAL).

25 April 2013

My blog post

Some people view depression as selfishness. I can completely understand how someone who has not experienced severe depression might see it like this. The victim cannot help but think of much else other than themselves and how hard and horrendous everything is for them at that stage in time. HOWEVER, depression is ACTUALLY a chemical imbalance in the brain. It is NOT selfish. NO ONE should feel guilty for feeling depressed, no matter who they are.

Statistics show that one in three people experience some form of depression during their life. This is not surprising with the current economy, lack of jobs, media pressure . . . everyday struggles building up. YES, there are people far worse off with incurable illnesses, in poverty, who have been through the most horrific things. But even though there is always someone worse off, ANYONE can have depression, bar none. It is the chemicals that cause it and no one should feel ashamed to speak to someone about it.

Perhaps I should (again) take some of my own advice. I KNOW how lucky I am. I know I am surrounded with love and have everything I need and more! I have written about it often and am always as grateful as ever for it. I am writing this because I am ashamed of myself for regularly experiencing the thought and feeling that it is easier to hide away and not face the world, or yourself. And often it is embarrassing admitting that you feel so low when you have so much. I think it is important for people to know that they are not alone. It always feels like you are, but you aren't. If one in three people experience it at some point then you would be surprised how many other people can relate to you.

29 April 2013

My blog post

I still have absolutely no clue what I want to do or who I'd like to be. I feel really stuck. I'm tired of being let down, and more so of letting myself down, in a big way.

29 April 2013

My blog post

I would give ALL of my limbs . . .

To go back three years, right now. No exaggeration.

5 May 2013

My blog post

Where the fuck is this light that's supposed to be at the end of this never-ending tunnel?

26 May 2013

My blog post

I feel like I never get anything to show for the hard work I DO put in. All the effort goes unnoticed. All the negatives are highlighted, as with anything really. But it's really annoying because I am doing as much as I can to get somewhere. It's exhausting and disappointing and I hate people thinking I don't try. BECAUSE I DO.

Yeah, rant over.

10 March 2014

This collection of information demonstrates just how far I have come, through my own strength, and with the unconditional love and support of my family and close friends.

After a summer spent writing and gaining some motivation through that, I managed to secure a job in Brighton. I moved out of my parents' home, and into a flat by the sea with my best friend. I got a cat named Mixie, who has helped me more than she will ever know!

Moving out was a massive step for me, as it gave me back my independence, and gave me the opportunity to be a normal 22-year-old girl. My parents' house was, and always will be, a very difficult place for me to be. I am haunted by painful memories, and see clear visions of myself brutally self-destructing in every room of the house.

In some ways life after an eating disorder, or during recovery from one, can be just as traumatic, scary and difficult as living with the disorder itself. I have had to grow up all over again, physically and mentally, which in some ways I have found humiliating. I have had to rediscover who I was before the illness, and attempt to work out who I am now. I was not confident with my body before, and neither am I now, so trying to reconnect with the world, and trying to be myself – whoever that may be – has been extremely challenging.

Most people I know, know what happened to me; which in turn created a difficult label for me to be able to shake off. I am constantly aware of what people's opinions may be of my current weight – whether people think I have gained too much – and how people consider me as a person. I have had to change my life and start over because of what happened, and sometimes I worry that people think I use this illness as an excuse for certain behaviours of things that I do even now. I want to take this opportunity to explain that that could not be further from the truth. It has been pure trial and error, leaps and falls, good intentions and mistakes, in order to get to where I am now. I still don't know myself completely, but I know that I am compassionate towards other people, and would never ever mean to cause harm or pain to another person. I did all that to myself instead!

When reading some of the brutally disturbing letters and messages that I wrote to my family, I feel physically sick, because at the time, that was how I thought. I was deadly serious in what I wrote. I put them through agony, and can only tell them how sorry I am, and dedicate this to them. Mum, Dad, brother and sister, I love you all and am eternally sorry for all the pain I caused you.

Although I lost almost everything through this cruel disease, I did not lose the people who matter the most: my family . . . and I did not lose my life. Looking back to that first letter from my mum, I cannot believe that I am here today, how far I have come, and how much I have been through that I will never be able to explain. In the darkest of times I believed recovery was utterly pointless, and I did not mind the thought of death, I would rather be dead than get fat/lose control/be in this world. I remember looking in the mirror when I was very ill and being completely mesmerized by my body, tracing my bones with my eyes, my head filled with sparkles and mist; I was in another realm, another world, dizzy with ideas and completely absorbed in thoughts. I am shocked to this day that recovery is possible, and that I got myself out from that black hole I was magnetically sucked into.

To look back and remember the feeling of falling will be with me forever, but luckily the human mind has a clever way of disguising and blanking out painful memories, and replacing them with the positivity that life has to offer. Time really is a healer.

I hope soxcthat this collection of thoughts, letters and messages can help others to see just how tangled emotions can become when this cruel disease overtakes the brain. I also hope that it can show the family and friends of sufferers how important their support is, even if they don't feel appreciated, or if they feel helpless.

To those who are suffering from anorexia, bulimia or ednos, or are currently trying to recover, the first steps genuinely are the hardest, and it is some journey ... However, when you start to rediscover the beauty of life, and what it has to offer, you will be amazed, and it is so worth it. It is not easy to get better, but it is possible, trust me. This is something I never thought I would type, but I am better, and I believe it.